Idioms in American Life

Julie Howard

The Language Institute
National College of Education
Chicago, Illinois

Illustrations by Pawel Bodytko

Prentice Hall Regents, Englewood Cliffs, NJ 07632

Library of Congress Cataloging-in-Publication Data

Howard, Julie, 1951–
   Idioms in American life.

   Includes index.
   1. Americanisms. 2. English language—Idioms.
3. English language—Text-books for foreign speakers.
I. Title.
PE2827.H68   1986   428.3′4   86–11263
ISBN 0–13–450207–8

Cover art: Pawel Bodytko
Cover design: Lundgren Graphics, Ltd.
Manufacturing buyer: Harry P. Baisley

Printed in the United States of America

30   29   28   27   26   25   24   23

ISBN 0-13-450207-8

Contents

To the Teacher

ABOUT THE BOOK

This introductory book of idioms is designed to be used in advanced-beginning and intermediate classes of ESL/EFL and is appropriate for adult, college-level, or secondary school students.

An idiom is a group of two or more words that has a special meaning different from the meanings of its component parts. The idioms in this book have been selected with regard to frequency of use and degree of difficulty. The lesson design is based on the following premises:

1. Advanced beginners and intermediate students have encountered idioms and are curious about them.
2. These students can and should learn to understand and use idioms.
3. To attain fluency learners must come away from the lesson with a clear understanding of the idioms in both situational and grammatical contexts.
4. A feeling of accomplishment will result when students have had intensive practice in the use of a few idioms at a time. Memorization of long lists of idioms that they cannot use confidently will result in discouragement and apathy.

The text consists of twenty self-contained lessons. There is a review section after every four lessons, and a crossword puzzle follows lessons 10 and 20.

The book will reinforce students' grammar, writing, and conversation skills. Manipulation of statements, questions, and negatives in the simple present, present continuous, simple past, and future tenses is required throughout. As a rule, items requiring familiarity with the present perfect are located in the second half of the book.

ORGANIZATION OF THE LESSONS

Each lesson presents five idioms and is divided into six sections:

I. *Dialogue.* The dialogues in which the idioms are introduced are adult in content and illustrative of real-life situations. Each is entitled with an expression or proverb that is explained in the appendix. Each dialogue consists of seven parts and is short enough to be memorized.

II. *Definitions.* Definitions are not given in the lessons so that students may have opportunities to guess meanings through the context of the dialogues. Definitions are listed in the index/glossary at the back of the book in the simplest terms possible without compromising the meaning.

III. *Notes.* These offer clarification and practical points to be considered in the use of the idioms.

IV. *Structure Practice.*   Exercises reinforce grammar skills while increasing familiarity with the uses of the idioms. Words in parentheses make students aware of possible changes in form.
 V. *Comprehension.*   This section tests learners' understanding of the idioms after their exposure to them in preceding parts of the lesson.
VI. *More Practice.*   These exercises allow students to use the idioms according to their own abilities and life experiences.

Each lesson, presented in its entirety, will occupy approximately forty-five minutes of class time. Part or all of sections IV, V, and VI, however, can be assigned for homework, thus reducing the time expended in class.

HOW TO USE THE LESSONS

1. Read the dialogue aloud to your students. You may want a student to participate with you, or you may ask two students to read.
2. Try to elicit definitions of the idiom by asking comprehension questions about the dialogue. Students should be encouraged to guess meanings, and they may write the definitions in section II. Discuss the title and its relationship to the dialogue; then reread the dialogue, asking students to repeat after you or to practice in pairs.
3. Write each idiom on the chalkboard, using parentheses to indicate words capable of change in form.

      Example: (take one's) time

   Ask students to complete sentences requiring manipulation.

Cue	Response
I	take my time.
She	takes her time.
Yesterday we	took our time.

   This step may not be necessary after students have become familiar with the format of the exercises. At this stage you should point out the idiosyncrasies of the idioms, which are found in section III.
4. Sections IV and V can be completed by students in class. Afterward, write the answers on the board so that students may correct their errors. Any appropriate answer should be accepted. In some cases more than one may be correct.
5. Section VI may be used for class discussion, written practice, or both. Encourage students to use the idioms in their responses.

Before beginning a new lesson, take a few minutes to review the idioms introduced in the preceding one. Ask for definitions and sample sentences.

Lesson 1

I. DIALOGUE: Easier Said Than Done

Tom: **What's the matter?** You look upset.

Marco: I **give up!** I'll never learn the past tense of these verbs.

Tom: That's easy. Just add *ed* to make the past tense.

Marco: I mean the irregular verbs. You have to learn them **by heart.** The past of *go* is *went.* It's crazy!

Tom: Why don't you sleep with the grammar book under your pillow? Maybe that will help.

Marco: Don't **make fun of** me! This is serious. We're going to have a test next week.

Tom: I'm sorry. I'll help you **brush up on** those verbs.

II. DEFINITIONS

What's the matter?:

give up:

by heart:

make fun of:

brush up on:

III. NOTES

give up: This idiom is often followed by a gerund (verb + *ing*).

> *Example:* If you want to lose weight, you'll have to give up **eating** candy.

IV. STRUCTURE PRACTICE

Write the idioms in the spaces provided. Be sure the statements agree in person and tense. Some statements will be negative (−). You may change the form of the words in parentheses.

1. **What (be) the matter?**

   a. _____ with Helen last night? She was very quiet.

   b. _____ with William? He looks very sad.

2. **(give) up**

   a. My brother _____ smoking last year.

   (−)b. He tries very hard to learn English. He_____

   _____.

   c. Why _____ you _____ running? It was very good for you.

3. **by heart**

   a. I have read that poem so many times that I know it_____

   _____.

   b. An actor must learn his role _____.

4. **(make) fun of**

   a. I thought my new hat was beautiful, but my husband _____

      _____ it.

   b. Why _____ you _____
      Bill's southern accent? That wasn't very nice of you.

   c. Robert _____ modern art because he
      doesn't understand it.

5. **(brush) up on**

   a. He usually _____ grammar on the week-
      ends because he doesn't have much time during the week.

   b. _____ you help me _____
      idioms next week?

   c. I _____ my Spanish while I was in
      Mexico on vacation.

V. COMPREHENSION

Write the idioms from this lesson in the spaces provided. Be sure to use
the correct person and tense.

1. It's a good idea to learn your social security number_____

   _____.

2. I'm going to France next year. I'll have to_____

   _____ my French before I go.

3. Ann looks angry. _____ with her?

4. The comedian _____ the president's foreign policy on television last night.

5. The doctor told him to _____ drinking
   coffee and tea.

6. _____ with the oven? It burned my bread.

7. You should never _____ another person's religion.

8. John finally _____ after trying to find his dog for three days.

VI. MORE PRACTICE

Respond with complete sentences, using the idioms as often as possible.

1. What poem or song did you learn **by heart** when you were a child? Do you still remember it?

2. What is something you should **give up** doing?

3. What are you going to **brush up on** this weekend?

4. Children are not very nice sometimes. Was there someone the children **made fun of** when you were a child? Why did they **make fun of** that person?

5. Your friend tells you his car is in the garage for repairs. How can you ask him what the problem is?

Lesson 2

I. DIALOGUE: Like Father, Like Son

George: What a wonderful baby! And he certainly **takes after** me, doesn't he?

Kate: Oh, yes. He doesn't look like me **at all.** He has your eyes, your chin, your. . . .

George: Uh-oh! He's going to cry again!

Kate: **Take it easy,** George. He's only yawning. Besides, you can't **go to pieces** every time the baby cries. Your mother told me you only stopped crying to eat.

George: You're right. I shouldn't be so nervous. We'll have to **take turns** watching him when you go back to work.

Kate: Now he really is crying.

George: I guess he has my personality, too.

II. DEFINITIONS

take after:

at all:

take it easy:

go to pieces:

take turns:

III. NOTES

at all: This idiom usually is used for emphasis in negative statements and questions.

> *Examples:* I **couldn't** eat at all when I was sick.
> **Didn't** you eat anything at all?

take turns: This expression is often followed by a gerund (verb + *ing*).

> *Example:*   My mother and aunt take turns **making** our Thanksgiving dinners.

IV. STRUCTURE PRACTICE

Write the idioms in the spaces provided. Be sure the statements agree in person and tense. Some statements will be negative (−). You may change the form of the words in parentheses.

1. **(take) after**

   a. She _____ her mother in both appearance and personality.

   (−)b. Paul _____ anyone in the family.

   c. When he was young, he _____ his mother, but now he looks more like his father.

2. **at all**

   a. Carl doesn't play the guitar _____ anymore.

   b. They don't eat meat _____. They're vegetarians.

3. **(take) it easy**

   a. We had a wonderful vacation. We really _____

      _____.

   b. He doesn't work very hard. He usually _____

      _____.

4. **(go) to pieces**

   a. When Barbara heard the news, she _____

      _____.

   b. He _____ every time someone in the family is sick.

   (−)c. Ann _____ when she lost her job. She was very calm.

5. **(take) turns**

   a. It was an easy trip. My brother and I _____
      _____ driving.

   b. Betty always _____ cleaning the house with her sister.

   c. We _____ cooking dinner next week.

V. COMPREHENSION

Write the idioms from this lesson in the spaces provided. Be sure to use the correct person and tense.

1. Jane _____ when her father died.

2. His doctor told him to _____.

3. Frank _____ his grandfather. They're both very good musicians.

4. The children have only one bicycle. They have to _____

   _____ using it.

5. _____, Sally! You don't have to drive so
   fast.

6. I don't speak Russian _____.

7. There aren't enough computers for all the students, so they'll have to

   _____.

8. I look like my father. I _____ him.

VI. MORE PRACTICE

Respond with complete sentences, using the idioms as often as possible.

1. What do you like to do when you **take it easy**?

2. Whom do you **take after**? In what ways?

3. What are some things you don't do **at all**?

4. Describe a situation in which you **take** (or **took**) **turns** doing something
   with someone else.

5. Describe a situation in which you or someone you know **went to pieces.**

Lesson 3

I. DIALOGUE: Getting in Shape

Joe: Would you like to play volleyball with us this weekend?

Dave: I'd love to, but **I'm** really **out of shape.** I haven't exercised much all winter.

Joe: That's okay. None of us are professionals.

Dave: How often do you play?

Joe: **Every other** Saturday. We**'d rather** play more often, but it's difficult to find a time when everyone can **get together.**

Dave: What time do you begin?

Joe: At 9:00. I'll **look forward to** seeing you then.

II. DEFINITIONS

be out of shape:

every other:

would rather:

get together:

look forward to:

III. NOTES

be out of shape: The opposite is **be in shape.**

Example: He**'s in shape** because he runs every day.

Related idioms are **stay in shape** and **get in shape.**

would rather: This phrase is followed by the simple form of the verb.

Example: He would rather **read** than **play** with the other children.

The contraction is **'d,** and the negative is **would rather not.**

Example: Ken wants to go to the movies, but I**'d rather not.**

look forward to: These words are often followed by a gerund (verb + *ing*).

Example: I'm looking forward to **having** some free time.

IV. STRUCTURE PRACTICE

Write the idioms in the spaces provided. Be sure the statements agree in person and tense. Some statements will be negative (−) and some will require contractions ('). You may change the form of the words in parentheses.

1. **(be) out of shape**

   a. Mary didn't play well because she_____

   _____.

   b. My brother should exercise more. He_____

   _____.

   c. You _____. You need to eat less and walk more.

2. **every other**

    a. The teacher asked the students to sit in _____

    _____ seat during the exam.

    b. She works in her uncle's shop _____
    Monday.

3. **(would) rather**

  (')a. She _____ have tea. She doesn't like
    coffee.

(')(−)b. I _____ play tennis today. It's too
    hot.

4. **(get) together**

    a. The whole family _____ at Bobby's
    birthday party last week.

    b. He _____ with his friends every week-
    end.

    c. _____ you _____
    with Steven next week?

5. **(look) forward to**

(−)a. I _____ going to the dentist.

    b. I'm _____ my vacation.

    c. He's _____ his graduation.

V. COMPREHENSION

Write the idioms from this lesson in the spaces provided. Be sure to use
the correct person and tense.

1. I don't wash my hair every day. I wash it _____

    _____ day.

2. I'm _____ seeing you.

3. Let's _____ for lunch tomorrow.

4. After his long illness, George _____.

5. They _____ eat at home than go to a restaurant.

6. The doctor told him he _____.

7. I always _____ receiving letters from my friends.

8. She couldn't decide if she _____ go to the opera or to the ballet.

VI. MORE PRACTICE

Respond with complete sentences, using the idioms as often as possible.

1. What do you usually do when you **get together** with your friends?

2. **Would** you **rather** go to Alaska or to Hawaii on vacation? Why?

3. What are you **looking forward to**?

4. Your friend is overweight and becomes tired easily. What's his problem? (Use **be out of shape.**) What should he do?

5. What's something you do **every other** day, week, or month?

Lesson 4

I. DIALOGUE: Robbing Peter to Pay Paul

Sam: How much money **have** you **got** today?

Frank: Oh, about twenty dollars. Why?

Sam: Well, **I'm broke** and I really need ten dollars. Could you lend it to me?

Frank: Why don't you ask your brother?

Sam: That's the problem. I borrowed ten dollars from him last month and now he wants his money **right away.**

Frank: Can't you see that borrowing from one person to pay another doesn't **make sense**? You **had better** learn to manage your money.

Sam: I guess you're right. Now, about that ten dollars?

II. DEFINITIONS

have got:

be broke:

right away:

make sense:

had better:

III. NOTES

have got: This idiom is used in the simple present tense only (American English). We can use **have got to** to mean **have to.**

Example: I **have got to** attend that meeting.

The contractions are **'s** (for he, she, it) and **'ve** (for I, we, you, they).

Example: I**'ve got** ten dollars and she**'s got** fifteen.

The negative forms are **hasn't** and **haven't.**

Example: They **haven't got** much money.

had better: This is a modal auxiliary and is followed by the simple form of the verb.

Example: I had better **go** to the bank before it closes.

It is used in the simple present tense only. The contraction is **'d** and the negative is **had better not.**

Example: You**'d better not** come to work late again.

IV. STRUCTURE PRACTICE

Write the idioms in the spaces provided. Be sure the statements agree in person and tense. Some statements will be negative (−) and some will require contractions ('). You may change the form of the words in parentheses.

1. **(have) got**

    a. How much money _____ he _____ ?

(')b. She _____ a lot of problems.

(−)c. "Would you lend me a pen?"

"I'm sorry, but I _____ one."

(−)d. He can't eat lunch today because he _____

_____ the time.

2. **(be) broke**

   a. He doesn't have any money. He _____ _____.

   b. We can't go to the movies because we _____

   _____.

   c. I stayed at home last weekend because I_____

   _____.

   d. Why _____ you _____
   last week? Did you pay a lot of bills?

3. **right away**

   a. I'm hungry. Let's eat _____.

   b. Please type that letter _____.

4. **(make) sense**

   a. That's a very good idea. It _____ _____.

(−)b. I didn't understand that book. It_____.

(−)c. I can't understand why Lisa is unhappy. It_____

_____.

5. **(had) better**

(−)a. You are sick. You _____ go to work
   today.

(')b. If we don't want to miss the beginning of the concert, we_____

_____ hurry.

V. COMPREHENSION

Write the idioms from this lesson in the spaces provided. Be sure to use the correct person and tense.

1. He wants you to call him _____. It's very important.

2. The Wilsons had to sell their car in order to pay their bills. They _____.

3. If you want to pass the test, you _____ study.

4. He _____ a house, but he doesn't have much furniture.

5. If you burn your hand, you should put it in cold water _____

   _____.

6. I liked the president's speech. It _____ a

   lot of _____.

7. They _____ a very nice apartment.

8. I _____ write a letter to my mother. I haven't written to her for a long time.

VI. MORE PRACTICE

Respond with complete sentences, using the idioms as often as possible.

1. Your friend is going to come to the United States next month. Make three sentences, telling him what he **had better** do to prepare for his trip.

2. What do you do when you**'re broke**?

3. Ask three classmates how much money they**'ve got** today. Write the answers.

4. Make three sentences, using **right away.**

5. Describe something about the English language that doesn't **make sense** to you.

Brush up on

Review: Lessons 1–4

I. Rewrite each of the ten sentences, changing the **boldface** words to idioms from the following list. Do not use the same idiom twice.

every other	**by heart**
(brush) up on	**(take) after**
would rather	**(take) it easy**
(give) up	**(be) broke**
right away	**(make) fun of**

1. Johnny has fallen down the stairs! Call an ambulance **immediately**!

   _____

2. I'm not very good at math. I need to **review** it.

   _____

3. **I am without money,** so I'll have to stay home tonight.

   _____

4. Joe **looks like** his mother.

   _____

5. The other children **laughed and joked about** Billy's haircut.

   _____

6. You must learn the irregular verbs **by memorization.**

   _____

7. Paul **prefers to** take the train. He says the bus is too slow.

   _____

8. Barbara had to **stop** jogging after she hurt her knee.

   _____

9. The club has a meeting **every alternate** Wednesday.

   _____

10. George works too hard. He should **relax.**

   _____

II. Use the following idioms to complete the exercises. Do not use the same idiom twice.

(look) forward to	**at all**
(have) got	**had better**
what (be) the matter	**(be) out of shape**
(make) sense	**(get) together**
(go) to pieces	**(take) turns**

A. Write idioms in the spaces provided.

   1. Mary _____ with her friends once a week to play cards.

   2. Frank _____ after his divorce and started drinking.

3. We are _____ to the party next Friday.

4. It _____ to exercise and eat a balanced diet.

5. I have a large family, so we have to _____ _____ using the bathroom in the morning.

B. Read the following situations and use idioms to make statements or questions.

1. Your friend is crying and you don't know why. What can you ask her?

   _____

2. You would like to know how many children your friend has. What question can you ask?

   _____

3. Your friend has a toothache. Tell him what he should do.

   _____

4. You are not in good physical condition. Make a statement about yourself.

   _____

5. You don't know one of word of Arabic. Make a statement about yourself.

   _____

Lesson 5

I. DIALOGUE: A Question of Money

Brian: Where would you like to go for dinner tonight?

Joan: Well, there's a new French restaurant downtown, or we can go to the seafood place on Lincoln Avenue. What do you think?

Brian: It**'s up to you.** Whatever you say is fine with me.

Joan: You should choose the restaurant if you're going to **foot the bill.**

Brian: Actually, I thought we could **go Dutch** this evening. I don't have much money.

Joan: Oh. **On second thought,** let's go to Hamburger Heaven. I haven't been there for a long time.

Brian: That's a great idea. That way we won't have to **dress up.**

II. DEFINITIONS

be up to someone:

foot the bill:

go Dutch:

on second thought:

dress up:

III. NOTES

foot the bill: Foot is treated as a regular verb, thus the past tense form is **footed.**

> *Example:* The army **footed** the bill for Joe's training as a radio operator.

IV. STRUCTURE PRACTICE

Write the idioms in the spaces provided. Be sure the statements agree in person and tense. Some statements will be negative (−). You may change the form of the words in parentheses.

1. **(be) up to (someone)**

   a. We can't help Joe. It _____ to stop drinking so much.

   b. I'm the only one in my family who can cook. It_____

   _____ to make dinner.

   c. Elizabeth drove, so it _____ to decide what time we left.

2. **(foot) the bill**

   a. Jane got married last year and her father_____

   _____.

   b. Harry always _____ when we go to a restaurant.

   (−)c. Jim invited his friends to the restaurant, but he_____

   _____.

3. **(go) Dutch**

   a. We each paid our own check at the nightclub. We _____

   _____.

   b. _____ you _____,
or did your friend pay for the tickets?

4. **on second thought**

   a. _____, we decided to take the bus instead of the train.

   b. Bill agreed to the plan _____.

5. **(dress) up**

   a. He always _____ for work.

   b. We _____ and went dancing last Saturday night.

(−)c. He _____. He likes to wear blue jeans.

V. COMPREHENSION

Write the idioms from this lesson in the spaces provided. Be sure to use the correct person and tense.

1. John and Mary usually _____ because neither of them has much money.

2. I was going to go to the party, but _____,
I decided to stay home.

3. I have to ask my boss if I can leave early. It _____

_____.

4. Ed feels uncomfortable in a suit. He never _____

_____.

5. The taxpayers _____ for public education in the United States.

6. Pam _____ for the party. She wore a long pink dress and a lot of jewelry.

7. It _____ the jury to decide if he's innocent or guilty.

8. She changed her opinion _____.

VI. MORE PRACTICE

Respond with complete sentences, using the idioms as often as possible.

1. In what situations do you usually **dress up**? What do you wear when you **dress up**?

2. Who usually **foots the bill** for a wedding in your country?

3. Do you think it's a good idea for a man and a woman to **go Dutch**? Why or why not?

4. Tell about a decision or opinion that you changed **on second thought.**

5. Make two statements, using **be up to someone.**

Lesson 6

I. DIALOGUE: Family Feud

Alice: Are you going to visit your in-laws on your vacation?

Susan: I'm afraid not. My husband just doesn't **get along with** his older brother.

Alice: Oh, really? Why not?

Susan: Poor Steve **does his best** to be pleasant, but they disagree about everything—politics, religion, sports, even the weather!

Alice: That's too bad. Do they **lose their tempers**?

Susan: Yes, they do. Sometimes they become very angry when they don't **see eye to eye.**

Alice: Well, don't worry too much. Brothers often argue. I'm sure they'll **make up** soon.

II. DEFINITIONS

get along with:

do one's best:

lose one's temper:

see eye to eye:

make up:

III. NOTES

get along with: When this idiom is at the end of a statement or question, it is simply **get along.**

> *Example:* Carl and his sister don't **get along.**

lose one's temper: When the subject is plural, **temper** becomes **tempers.**

> *Example:* **We** don't often lose **our tempers.**

IV. STRUCTURE PRACTICE

Write the idioms in the spaces provided. Be sure the statements agree in person and tense. Some statements will be negative (−). You may change the form of the words in parentheses.

1. **(get) along with**

   a. He likes his job and he _____ _____ his boss.

(−)b. She moved because she and her roommate_____

   _____.

(−)c. I don't visit my cousin very often because I_____

   _____ her.

2. **(do one's) best**

   a. We _____ to arrive on time every day.

   b. They _____, but they didn't win the game.

(−)c. He's very intelligent, but he _____ in school.

3. **(lose one's) temper(s)**

  a. He never _____. He's a very calm person.

(−)b. Please _____. I'm only joking.

  c. Mrs. Green _____ when the dogs ruined her garden.

4. **(see) eye to eye**

(−)a. Lucy and Fred decided not to get married because they_____

_____ on many things.

  b. My mother and I almost always agree. She_____

_____ with me.

5. **(make) up**

  a. _____ you _____ with your friend after your argument on Saturday night?

  b. He often argues with his brother, but he always_____

_____ with him.

V. COMPREHENSION

Write the idioms from this lesson in the spaces provided. Be sure to use the correct person and tense.

1. John and Mary are a perfect couple. They_____

_____ on everything.

2. Romeo and Juliet had a terrible fight, but later they kissed and_____

_____.

3. My sister _____ and shouted at the children.

4. The students _____ to answer the questions correctly.

5. Richard and Paul _____ on politics. They are both members of the Democratic party.

6. I enjoy being with Amy. I _____ her very well.

7. I _____, but still I'm not a very good cook.

8. The two drivers _____ after the accident and began to fight.

VI. MORE PRACTICE

Respond with complete sentences, using the idioms as often as possible.

1. When was the last time you **lost your temper**? Why did you **lose your temper?**

2. a. Whom do you **get along with**? Why?

   b. Whom don't you **get along with**? Why not?

3. You had a terrible argument with your friend, but now you're sorry. How will you **make up** with him/her?

4. What things do you think a husband and wife should **see eye to eye** on?

5. In what situations do you **do your best**?

Lesson 7

I. DIALOGUE: A Man of His Word

Ralph: Can I **count on you** to help me move next Saturday?

Gary: No problem. What time?

Ralph: About 8:00. Are you sure you can come?

Gary: I'll be there. Don't worry.

Ralph: You know, the last time you offered to help me, you **showed up** three hours after we had finishcd.

Gary: I didn't come late **on purpose**. I overslept. I won't **let you down** this time.

Ralph: Thanks. I really need your help. And please **let me know** if you're going to be late.

II. DEFINITIONS

count on someone:

show up:

on purpose:

let someone down:

let someone know:

III. NOTES

count on someone: This idiom is often followed by the infinitive (*to* + verb).

   Example: I can count on my sister **to lend** me money.

IV. STRUCTURE PRACTICE

Write the idioms in the spaces provided. Be sure the statements agree in person and tense. Some statements will be negative (−). You may change the form of the words in parentheses.

1. **(count) on (someone)**

   a. Fred is very irresponsible. I can't_____

      _____.

   b. I help the elderly woman next door. She_____

      _____ to cut her grass in the summer.

   c. She _____ her sister to drive her to
      work last week.

2. **(show) up**

(−)a. I waited for an hour, but Bob _____.

   b. Barbara finally _____ at 10:00 last
      night.

   c. Bill usually _____ here around 9:00 in
      the morning.

3. **on purpose**

   a. He set fire to the house _____ in order
      to collect the insurance money.

   b. The neighbor was very angry because he thought the boys had

      broken his window _____.

4. **(let someone) down**

    a. Jane really _____. She didn't come to my party.

(−)b. Andrew _____. He's always ready to help me.

    c. We were unhappy because our team didn't play well. They_____

    _____.

5. **(let someone) know**

    a. Your mother called. She wants you to_____

    _____ if you're going to come for dinner on Saturday.

    b. I'm not sure if I will be able to come to the meeting, but I _____ next week.

    c. I don't understand why John is angry. I _____ _____ that I couldn't meet him.

V. COMPREHENSION

Write the idioms from this lesson in the spaces provided. Be sure to use the correct person and tense.

1. Please don't be angry. I didn't wreck your car_____

    _____.

2. Martin always _____ late for class.

3. Mary wants you to _____ when you finish talking on the phone. She would like to use it.

4. Dan's parents wanted him to finish high school, but he quit. He

    _____.

5. I expect our guests to _____ about 7:30.

6. David is my best friend. I can _____ to listen to my problems.

7. The police think that it was murder and that someone pushed the woman out the window _____.

8. The mayor promised to improve the parks, but he_____

_____ the voters _____.

VI. MORE PRACTICE

Respond with complete sentences, using the idioms as often as possible.

1. Describe a situation in which someone **let you down**.

2. Whom do you usually **count on** to help you? In what ways?

3. Your friend is coming for a visit and would like you to meet him at the airport. What does he have to **let you know**?

4. Do you know someone who is often late? Describe a situation in which this person **showed up** late.

5. You accidentally took your classmate's book home with you. How can you apologize, using **on purpose**?

Lesson 8

I. DIALOGUE: Duty Calls

Elizabeth: Would you **drop this dress off** at the dry cleaner for me?

Matthew: Okay, but it's a little **out of my way**. Can I do it tomorrow?

Elizabeth: Yes, but if you take it today, I'll be able to **pick it up** on Saturday morning. I'd like to have it **in time** for the wedding.

Matthew: Wedding? What wedding?

Elizabeth: Don't you remember? Your niece Sylvia is going to get married on Saturday.

Matthew: Oh, no! That's the day of the championship football game. I had to buy tickets a month **in advance**.

Elizabeth: That's too bad, but surely you can see that the wedding is more important. Sylvia is going to get married only once—we hope!

II. DEFINITIONS

drop off:

out of one's way:

pick up:

in time:

in advance:

III. NOTES

drop off: This idiom is a separable two-word verb.

> *Examples:* The bus **drops off** Jane at the corner.
> The bus **drops** Jane **off** at the corner.

When a pronoun is used, the verb must be separated.

> *Example:* The bus **drops** her **off** at the corner.

pick up: This is also a separable two-word verb and behaves the same as **drop off**.

in time: When this is followed by a verb, the infinitive (*to* + verb) is used.

> *Example:* I didn't get home in time **to watch** that program on TV.

When **in time** is followed by a noun, the preposition *for* is used.

> *Example:* I didn't arrive in time **for that program**.

IV. STRUCTURE PRACTICE

Write the idioms in the spaces provided. Be sure the statements agree in person and tense. Some statements will be negative (−). You may change the form of the words in parentheses.

1. **(drop someone/something) off—(drop) off (someone/something)**

    a. These shoes need to be repaired. I'll _____

       _____ at the shoe repair shop.

    b. The taxi driver _____ at the corner and we walked two blocks to the theater.

    c. Will you _____ the boys _____ at the park before you go to work?

d. The teacher asked us to _____ our

papers _____ in her office when we finish them.

2. **out of (one's) way**

   a. Thank you for the ride. I hope you didn't have to go_____

   _____.

   b. Because the road we usually take was closed for repairs, we had to

   drive miles _____.

   c. I can take the books back to the library for you. It isn't_____

   _____.

3. **(pick someone/something) up—(pick) up (someone/something)**

   a. I _____ my children _____
   after school every day.

(−)b. I'm angry with Pete. He _____ yesterday. He said he forgot.

   c. The eye doctor called to say that my new glasses are ready. Can you

   _____ for me?

   d. My brother _____ after work and took
   me home.

4. **in time**

   a. We set the alarm clock for 4:00 A.M. because we wanted to get up

   _____ to see the sunrise.

   b. Greg didn't arrive at the airport _____
   for the 1:00 flight. He had to wait for the next one.

5. **in advance**

   a. It's a good idea to make hotel reservations_____

   _____.

   b. Most people who live in apartments have to pay their rent a month

   _____.

V. COMPREHENSION

Write the idioms from this lesson in the spaces provided. Be sure to use the correct person and tense.

1. Carolyn arrived at school _____ to have a cup of coffee before class.

2. On Friday I took the film to the drugstore to be developed. The clerk told me I could _____ the pictures on Monday.

3. When I went shopping with my grandmother, I_____ _____ at the entrance of the store before I parked the car.

4. My dentist is so busy that I have to make an appointment with her six weeks _____.

5. I rarely shop at MacMillan's Department Store. It's_____ _____.

6. John didn't want to go to the post office because it was_____ _____.

7. Sally did her homework quickly because she wanted to finish_____ _____ for her favorite television program.

8. When Mrs. Jordan was sick, I made some soup for her and_____ _____ at her house.

VI. MORE PRACTICE

Respond with complete sentences, using the idioms as often as possible.

1. Make three sentences about things you do, or did, **in advance**.

2. What things do you arrive **in time** to do before class?

3. First you went to Larry's house. Then you took him to work in your car. Describe this situation, using **pick up** and **drop off**.

4. You took your watch to the repair shop on Monday. On Thursday you went back to the repair shop and took your watch home. Describe this situation, using **drop off** and **pick up**.

5. Your friend asks for a ride home in your car. What can you say, using **out of one's way**?

See eye to eye

Review: Lessons 5–8

I. Complete the following conversations, using idioms from the list below and other words if necessary. Do not use the same idiom twice.

(get) along with	**(foot) the bill**
(see) eye to eye	**in time**
(show) up	**(make) up**
on purpose	**(dress) up**
(pick) up	**(let someone) know**

1. A: "What time did your sister arrive for dinner?"

   B: "She finally ＿＿＿＿＿＿＿＿＿＿＿＿＿＿＿＿＿＿＿＿＿＿＿."

2. A: "Who paid for Joe's graduation party?"

   B: "His parents ＿＿＿＿＿＿＿＿＿＿＿＿＿＿＿＿＿＿＿＿＿＿＿."

3. A: "Did you leave the door open accidentally?"

   B: "No, I ＿＿＿＿＿＿＿＿＿＿＿＿＿＿＿＿＿＿＿＿＿＿＿＿＿＿＿."

4. A: "I'll need a ride home after work tomorrow."

   B: "Okay, I'll ＿＿＿＿＿＿＿＿＿＿＿＿＿＿＿＿＿＿＿＿＿＿＿＿."

5. A: "Do you like your mother-in-law?"

   B: "Yes, I ＿＿＿＿＿＿＿＿＿＿＿＿＿＿＿＿＿＿＿＿＿＿＿＿＿＿."

6. A: "Why does he always wear a suit and tie?"

   B: "Because he likes to ＿＿＿＿＿＿＿＿＿＿＿＿＿＿＿＿＿＿＿＿."

7. A: "I heard that John and Sue had a terrible argument."

   B: "Yes, but _____."

8. A: "Do you and Fred agree on politics?"

   B: "No, we _____."

9. A: "You should tell them you won't be able to go to the party."

   B: "Okay, I'll _____."

10. A: "Did you have time to eat breakfast before you left for work?"

   B: "Yes, I got up _____."

II. Use the following idioms to make statements that have similar meanings. Do not use the same idiom twice.

(let someone) down	**in advance**
(count) on (someone)	**out of (one's) way**
(lose one's) temper	**(do one's) best**
(go) Dutch	**(be) up to (someone)**
on second thought	**(drop) off**

1. He bought the tickets three weeks before the concert.

   _____

2. She became very angry.

   _____

3. We tried very hard.

   _____

4. They disappointed us.

   _____

5. We can depend on Steve.

_____

6. We each paid for our own dinner.

_____

7. It's Mary's decision.

_____

8. He changed his plans after thinking again.

_____

9. I took the books to the library yesterday.

_____

10. The hardware store is very far from where I'm going.

_____

Lesson 9

I. DIALOGUE: A Foot in the Door

Judy: Hi, Gloria. I'm glad you called. I **was about to** call you.

Gloria: Really? Why?

Judy: I **found out** there's a job opening for an accountant in the company where I work. I thought you might be interested in it.

Gloria: I am. I'll call tomorrow morning and make an appointment for an interview.

Judy: You should **get in touch with** Mr. Prescott. He**'s in charge of** the accounting department.

Gloria: Thanks for telling me about the job.

Judy: I'm happy to help. **After all,** what are friends for?

II. DEFINITIONS

be about to:

find out:

get in touch with:

be in charge of:

after all:

III. NOTES

be in charge of: This idiom is often followed by a gerund (verb + *ing*).

>   *Example:*   The secretary is in charge of **ordering** supplies for the office.

IV. STRUCTURE PRACTICE

Write the idioms in the spaces provided. Be sure the statements agree in person and tense. Some statements will be negative (−). You may change the form of the words in parentheses.

1. **(be) about to**

    a. They _____ leave the house when the phone rang.

    b. The students are coming into the classroom. The class_____ _____ _____ begin.

    c. We're closing our books. We _____ _____ go home.

2. **(find) out**

    a. How _____ you _____ about the party? We wanted it to be a surprise.

    (−)b. He _____ about the job opening until it was too late.

    c. The boy's mother always _____ when he does something wrong.

3. **(get) in touch with**

    a. _____ you _____ Mary last night?

    b. My brother usually _____ me about
       once a month.

    c. I finally _____ her yesterday.

4. **(be) in charge of**

    a. Mrs. Jones _____ the sales department
       from 1970 to 1978.

    b. Who _____ answering the telephone in
       this office?

    c. I _____ buying food for the picnic.

5. **after all**

    a. I'm not surprised that Richard lost his job. _____
    _____, he was late for work almost
       every day.

    b. Please don't leave the party now. _____
    _____, it's only 10:00.

V. COMPREHENSION

Write the idioms from this lesson in the spaces provided. Be sure to use the correct person and tense.

1. Adam became very angry when he _____
   that his son had wrecked the car.

2. I'm going to ask my boss for a raise. _____,
   I've worked there for four years at the same pay.

3. I've been trying to _____ Greg all day. Do
   you know where he is?

4. The plane _____ take off when one of the
   engines caught fire.

5. The treasurer of an organization _____
   the money.

6. The dog _____ eat the roast when Mrs. Collins came in and saved it.

7. When did you _____ that your wife is going to have a baby?

8. I should _____ Marilyn. I haven't talked to her in a long time.

VI. MORE PRACTICE

Respond with complete sentences, using the idioms as often as possible.

1. How did you **find out** about the English classes at your school?

2. a. I have just put the food on the table. Now, I'm sitting down. What **am** I **about to** do?

   b. You've just put on your pajamas. Now you're turning off the light. What **are** you **about to** do?

3. How can I **get in touch with** you this weekend?

4. Your friend has been studying English for six months. He's unhappy because English is still very difficult for him. What can you say, using **after all**, to make him feel better?

5. a. Who's **in charge of** the English classes at your school?

   b. Your class is going to have a party. Who do you think should **be in charge of** buying the food?

Lesson 10

I. DIALOGUE: First Things First

Toni: That teacher always **finds fault with** my compositions. I spent a lot of time on this one last week and now he wants me to **do it over**.

Janet: What's the problem?

Toni: Some small mistakes—that's all. Look at my paper.

Janet: These spelling errors do **stand out**. There shouldn't be a *y* in *studies,* and you forgot the second *p* in *stopped.*

Toni: **I'm** not **to blame**. It's this crazy language! In my language, the spelling is very regular.

Janet: English has a few basic rules, too. You'll **be better off** if you learn them.

Toni: It might be easier to go back to my country!

II. DEFINITIONS

find fault with:

do something over:

stand out:

be to blame:

be better off:

III. NOTES

do something over: More specific verbs are often substituted for *do*.

> *Examples:* The secretary **typed** the letter over.
> The book was so good that I **read** it over.

I. STRUCTURE PRACTICE

Write the idioms in the spaces provided. Be sure the statements agree in person and tense. Some statements will be negative (−). You may change the form of the words in parentheses.

1. **(find) fault with**

   a. Why _____ you always _____

   _____   _____ my driving? I'm very careful.

   (−)b. Jane is very popular because she _____
   other people.

   c. I liked the movie, but Sam _____   _____ it.
   He thought it was boring.

2. **(do something) over**

   a. The boss found some mistakes in the reports, so she asked Mike to

   _____.

   b. I didn't iron my shirt very well the first time, so now I'm_____

   _____.

   c. Andy _____ the work _____
   because he wanted it to be perfect.

3. **(stand) out**

   a. Margaret is so beautiful that she _____
   in a crowd.

b. Robert really _____ in high school. He was an excellent student and a great athlete.

c. We underline the important words so they will_____

_____.

4. **(be) to blame**

a. John _____ for the accident. He was driving too fast.

b. Peter thinks the president _____ for unemployment.

(−)c. Parents _____ always _____ for their children's bad behavior.

5. **(be) better off**

a. Nick _____ now that he has a full-time job.

b. The city _____ when Harold Cooper was mayor.

V. COMPREHENSION

Write the idioms from this lesson in the spaces provided. Be sure to use the correct person and tense.

1. I don't like Bob. He _____ everything I do.

2. Both countries say the other _____ for starting the war.

3. When I looked through the telescope, one very bright star _____

_____ from the others.

4. It's easy to _____ Charles. He's lazy and impolite.

5. Teachers use white chalk because it _____ on the blackboard.

6. Chris and Brenda _____ when they lived in the country. They aren't happy in the city.

7. The other children said that Scott _____ for the broken window.

8. Tom lost his homework, so he had to_____

    _____.

VI. MORE PRACTICE

Respond with complete sentences, using the idioms as often as possible.

1. **Are** you **better off** now than you were five years ago? Why or why not?

2. In your opinion, who or what **is to blame** for most crime?

3. Did your parents sometimes **find fault with** you when you were a child? Why?

4. Describe a situation in which you **did something over**.

5. Use **stand out** in two sentences.

Crossword Puzzle: Lessons 1–10

ACROSS

1. An actor must learn his lines by _____.
3. I get along _____ my roommate very well.
6. What time did Peter finally _____ up?
7. Helen found _____ with my idea, but she didn't have one of her own.
9. We really should get rid _____ those old newspapers.
10. Bob and I _____ together for lunch once a week.
12. We always argue about politics because we just don't _____ eye to eye.
14. They usually _____ Dutch when they eat in a restaurant.
15. I'm out of _____. I need to exercise more.
16. Please let me _____ when your train will arrive so I can meet you at the station.
18. I made so many mistakes on that letter that I had to do it _____.
19. He gets a paycheck _____ other week.

DOWN

1. John made up _____ mind to move to Texas.
2. I was _____ to call Jerry when he called me.

4. It's your birthday. It _____ _____ to you to decide where you'd like to go.
5. I'm a lot better _____ now than I was five years ago.
8. We got there in _____ to buy popcorn before the movie began.
9. _____ second thought I decided to stay home last night.
10. Elizabeth _____ to pieces when she hears about new fighting in Nagarubia. Her son is a soldier there.
11. I know you will _____ your best to learn English.
12. I don't understand this sentence. It doesn't make _____.
13. It's not nice to _____ fun of other people.
14. You can _____ in touch with me at 577-9834.
17. I rarely go downtown. It's out of my _____.

Lesson 11

I. DIALOGUE: A Taste of His Own Medicine

Bill: How's your cousin Arthur? I haven't seen him for a long time.

Grace: He's in the hospital with pneumonia. It **was touch and go** for a while, but he's much better now.

Bill: I'm sorry to hear he's been sick. Isn't he a doctor?

Grace: Yes, and everyone knows that doctors are sometimes the worst patients. He's not **used to** staying in bed and he complains all the time.

Bill: Well, I hope he **gets over** it soon.

Grace: I'm sure the nurses will be happy when he's **up and about**, too.

Bill: I'll visit him tomorrow. Maybe he'll feel better if he has someone to **keep him company**.

II. DEFINITIONS

be touch and go:

be used to:

get over:

be up and about:

keep someone company:

III. NOTES

be used to: This idiom is often followed by a gerund (verb + *ing*).

    Example: He is used to **staying** in the best hotels.

be up and about: The phrase **be up and around** is used in similar situations.

    Example: Lillian **was up and around** the day after she had the baby.

IV. STRUCTURE PRACTICE

Write the idioms in the spaces provided. Be sure the statements agree in person and tense. Some statements will be negative (−). You may change the form of the words in parentheses.

1. **(be) touch and go**

    a. It _____, but our team finally won the game.

    b. Doug and Paula's romance _____. One day they're not speaking to each other, and the next day they're talking about marriage.

    c. Carla's condition after the operation_____

    _____ and her family was very worried.

2. **(be) used to**

    a. I _____ getting up early. I rarely sleep late.

(−)b. At first he didn't like Florida because he _____

    _____ hot weather.

    c. _____ you _____ your new job, or is it still difficult?

(−)d. I _____ holding babies. It makes me nervous.

3. **(get) over**

   a. Mr. Jensen hasn't _____ the death of his wife.

   b. He had a cold, but he _____ it quickly.

   (−)c. Jack _____ his divorce until he met Anne.

4. **(be) up and about**

   a. Jerry _____ three days after the accident. It was incredible.

   b. I'm happy to see that you _____ again.

   c. I thought you were still sick. How long have you _____

   _____?

5. **(keep someone) company**

   a. Martha was lonely while her husband was away, so we _____

   _____.

   b. Many people have pets to _____.

   c. I'm not hungry, but if you want to go to a restaurant, I'll

   _____.

V. COMPREHENSION

Write the idioms from this lesson in the spaces provided. Be sure to use the correct person and tense.

1. I was very sick, but now I _____.

2. Rick is my best friend. He _____ when I need someone to talk to.

3. The first year of our business _____, but this year we're making money.

4. The doctor says that Diane will _____ in two or three weeks.

5. Maria _____ life in the United States now. She's been here for five years.

6. Brad was angry with me, but he _____ it and we're friends again.

7. The Millers _____ the country, and they don't like the noise and traffic in the city.

8. Time passes more quickly when you have someone to_____

   _____.

VI. MORE PRACTICE

Respond with complete sentences, using the idioms as often as possible.

1. When was the last time you were sick? How long did it take you to **get over** it?

2. After your last illness, what did you do when you **were up and about** again?

3. Make two sentences about yourself, using **be used to**.

4. Describe a situation that **was touch and go** for you.

5. Who usually **keeps you company** in your free time?

Lesson 12

I. DIALOGUE: Last-Minute Notice

Ron: Guess who I saw today?

Sue: Who?

Ron: Tom Porter. I **ran into** him at the post office.

Sue: I haven't seen him for ages. Is he still **going out** with that blonde?

Ron: No, he **fell in love** with someone he met at work and they're going to get married next month. **By the way**, I invited both of them to dinner this evening. They should be here in an hour.

Sue: Tonight! We**'re out of** bread, and butter, and coffee, and . . . !

Ron: Don't worry. I'll go to the supermarket while you start dinner.

II. DEFINITIONS

run into:

go out:

fall in love:

by the way:

be out of:

III. NOTES

be out of: The idiom **run out of** is similar. It means *to use all of something.*

> *Example:* My car **ran out of** gas and I had to walk to the nearest gas
> station.

IV. STRUCTURE PRACTICE

Write the idioms in the spaces provided. Be sure the statements agree in person and tense. Some statements will be negative (−). You may change the form of the words in parentheses.

1. **(run) into**

   a. She often _____ someone she knows at the supermarket.

   b. "I saw Betty downtown yesterday." "Oh, really? Where_____

      you _____ her?"

2. **(go) out**

   a. Jane _____ with Roger every weekend.

   (−)b. I _____ last weekend. I had to work.

   (−)c. He _____ very much. He likes to stay home.

3. **(fall) in love**

   a. Frank _____ with a different girl every week.

   b. I _____ with you the moment I met you.

   c. Sally has never _____.

4. **by the way**

   a. Please come to Jim's birthday party. _____

   _____, it's a surprise, so don't mention
   it to him.

   b. Here are your keys. I found them under your hat, _____

   _____.

5. **(be) out of**

   a. I have to go to the gas station. The car _____

   almost _____ gas.

   b. We _____ aspirin, so I had to go to the
   drugstore.

   c. I'm sorry but we _____ that book. We
   sold the last one yesterday.

V. COMPREHENSION

Write the idioms from this lesson in the spaces provided. Be sure to use
the correct person and tense.

1. We usually don't _____ during the week
    because we have to get up early.

2. He _____ an old friend on the street the
    other day.

3. I read that book last year. _____, it was
    very interesting.

4. I can't make a cake because I _____ eggs.

5. Rachel likes to dance when she _____.

6. Many tourists _____ with Rome. It's a
    beautiful city.

7. We _____ sugar, so I made the dessert with honey.

8. "Darling, I think I'm _____ with you."

VI. MORE PRACTICE

Respond with complete sentences, using the idioms as often as possible.

1. What **are** you **out of**, or almost **out of**?

2. What do you like to do when you **go out**?

3. When was the last time you **ran into** someone you know? Where did you **run into** that person?

4. Have you ever **fallen in love**? With whom? How long did you know the person before you **fell in love**?

5. Rewrite the following sentences, adding **by the way**.

   a. I saw Fred yesterday. He's lost a lot of weight.

   b. I moved last week. I have a new telephone number.

   c. I talked to Lucy last night. She asked about you.

Fall in love

Review: Lessons 9–12

I. Match the numbers and letters to make statements using idioms. Write
   the statements below and underline the idioms.

1. It took her three weeks to
2. Mr. Peterson always finds fault with
3. The driver of the blue car
4. The receptionist
5. Joe's bright yellow tie
6. I was about to go to bed
7. It was touch and go, but
8. Jill didn't want
9. I was surprised to
10. I'm better off now

a. is in charge of taking messages.
b. the operation was successful.
c. really stood out.
d. to go out with Jack.
e. get over her cold.
f. that I have a job.
g. his wife's cooking.
h. find out that Joe was married.
i. when someone knocked on the door.
j. was to blame for the accident.

1. _____

2. _____

3. _____

4. _____

5. _____

6. _____

7. _____

8. _____

9. _____

10. _____

II. Use the idioms in the following list to complete the exercises. Do not use the same idiom twice.

(be) used to	**(fall) in love**
(get) in touch with	**by the way**
after all	**(do something) over**
(run) into	**(keep someone) company**
(be) out of	**(be) up and around**

A. Write the idioms in the blank spaces.

1. I tried to _____ Mr. Jones all day, but he wasn't at his home or at his office.

2. My parents _____ on their first date and got married two months later.

3. Please come to our house for dinner. _____

   _____, Kathy will be there too.

4. Why don't we have some champagne?_____

   _____, it's New Year's Eve.

5. Mrs. Johnson has three cats to _____

   _____.

B. Read the following situations and use idioms to make statements.

1. You have moved from a warm climate to a cold climate and you're uncomfortable because of the weather. What can you say about yourself?

2. You are the boss. One of your employees has just typed a letter for you. It is full of mistakes. What can you say to the employee?

3. You usually have milk with your cereal, but you don't have any milk today. Describe this situation.

4. Brian was sick in bed for two weeks, but now he's out of bed and walking around. What can you say about him?

5. You met Susan by chance at the post office today. What can you tell your friends?

Lesson 13

I. DIALOGUE: No One Is an Island

Ed: How do you like Chicago?

Maria: I haven't **made up my mind** yet. I've been here for only three months, you know. I'm a little homesick.

Ed: Where do you live?

Maria: On Kimball near Lawrence.

Ed: Oh, I **used to live** in that neighborhood. I still have **quite a few** friends there.

Maria: I haven't **made friends** with anyone. I'm a very shy person. It's difficult for me to talk to people I don't know.

Ed: Well, **keep trying**. People from Chicago are really friendly. I'll introduce you to some of my friends.

II. DEFINITIONS

make up one's mind:

used to (verb):

quite a few:

make friends:

keep (verb + *ing*):

III. NOTES

quite a few: This idiom is used with count nouns.

>   *Example:* I have quite a few **books** (**cousins**, **records**, **cans** of soup, etc.).

It is not used in negative statements. The negative form is **not many**.

>   *Example:* There are quite a few Chinese students in the class, but there are **not many** Indonesian students.

keep (verb + *ing*): The idiom **keep on (verb + *ing*)** has the same meaning and uses but is more informal.

>   *Example:* **Keep on walking** until you come to State Street.

IV. STRUCTURE PRACTICE

Write the idioms in the spaces provided. Be sure the statements agree in person and tense. Some statements will be negative (−). You may change the form of the words in parentheses.

1. **(make) up (one's) mind(s)**

    a. He _____ last night. He's going to ask Peggy to marry him.

    b. Peggy can't _____. Maybe she'll marry him, and maybe she won't.

(−)c. Don and JoAnn haven't decided what to have for dinner. They

    _____ .

2. **used to (verb)**

    a. Jim worked in a factory four years ago, but now he works in a department store. He _____ in a factory.

b. Carol was married, but now she's divorced. She_____

_____ married.

3. **quite a few**

a. There were _____ men at the party, but not very many women.

b. I saw _____ interesting paintings at the exhibition.

4. **(make) friends**

a. Barbara _____ everywhere she goes. She's very nice.

b. Frank _____ a lot of _____ when he was in college.

(−)c. I _____ easily. I'm shy.

5. **(keep) (verb + *ing*)**

a. He will continue to work there until he finds a better job. He will

_____ there.

b. She continues to make the same mistakes. She_____

_____ the same mistakes.

c. The children continued to play after their mother asked them to go

to bed. They _____.

V. COMPREHENSION

Write the idioms from this lesson in the spaces provided. Be sure to use the correct person and tense.

1. It's easy for Walter to _____. Everyone likes him.

2. He _____ fat, but now he's very thin.

3. There were _____ people at the zoo yesterday.

4. We can't _____. We might stay here, or we might move to Boston.

5. The children quickly _____ with the new boy and began to play.

6. You should _____ about that stereo. If you don't want to buy it, I'll sell it to someone else.

7. He didn't stop running when the police officer shouted at him. He

   _____.

8. I _____ my hair myself, but now I go to the barber.

VI. MORE PRACTICE

Respond with complete sentences, using the idioms as often as possible.

1. What do you do now that you are going to **keep doing** in the future?

2. Is it easy or difficult for you to **make friends**? Why?

3. Make three sentences, using **quite a few**.

4. What are some things you **used to do** that you don't do now?

5. What did you **make up your mind** to do recently?

Lesson 14

I. DIALOGUE: Potluck

Faye: Will I see you at Mike's picnic tomorrow?

Chris: Sure. Everyone will be there. What are you going to take?

Faye: Potato salad. I've already made it. **How about** you?

Chris: Oh, no! I was going to make potato salad **as well**. Now I'll have to **come up with** something else. One potato salad is enough.

Faye: Don't worry. You still have time to **think it over**.

Chris: Yes, and if it continues to rain like this, Mike might **call the picnic off**.

Faye: Don't say that! What will I do with twenty pounds of potato salad?

II. DEFINITIONS

how about:

as well:

come up with:

think over:

call off:

III. NOTES

how about: When this idiom is used in an informal suggestion, request, or offer, it is often followed by a gerund (verb + *ing*).

Example: How about **helping** me move the table?

think over: This is a separable two-word verb.

Examples: We really need to **think your idea over**.
We really need to **think over your idea**.

When a pronoun is used, the verb must be separated.

Example: We really need to **think it over**.

call off: This is also separable and behaves the same as **think over**.

IV. STRUCTURE PRACTICE

Write the idioms in the spaces provided. Be sure the statements agree in person and tense. Some statements will be negative (−). You may change the form of the words in parentheses.

1. **How about**

   a. _____ going to a movie this evening?

   b. I'm tired. _____ you?

   c. _____ another cup of coffee?

2. **as well**

   a. Thomas Jefferson was an architect, philosopher, and president of the United States _____.

   b. Tim wanted to go _____, but there wasn't room for him in the car.

c. We're on vacation in Colorado. We'd like to go to Arizona
_____, but I don't think we'll have
time.

3. **(come) up with**

    a. Susan _____ a good plan at the meet-
ing yesterday.

(−)b. I worked on that math problem for an hour, but I _____

_____ the answer.

4. **(think something) over—(think) over (something)**

    a. Paul _____ it _____

_____ and decided to move to California.

    b. We _____ your idea and will give you
our decision tomorrow.

5. **(call something) off—(call) off (something)**

(−)a. It was raining, but they _____ the race

_____.

    b. The union _____ the strike when the
company offered the workers more benefits.

    c. They _____ the wedding _____
because they decided not to get married.

V. COMPREHENSION

Write the idioms from this lesson in the spaces provided. Be sure to use
the correct person and tense.

1. Cheryl and Greg haven't _____ a name
for the baby yet. They can't find one they both like.

2. When they offered the job to Linda, she told them she had to

_____.

3. Carolyn is a good tennis player and an excellent skier_____
   _____.

4. _____ scrambled eggs for breakfast?

5. The school _____ all classes because of
   the terrible weather last week.

6. Julia has three children and a full-time job_____
   _____, so she's always busy.

7. The Carters _____ their trip to Florida
   when Mrs. Carter broke her leg.

8. I thought that book was very interesting._____
   _____ you?

VI. MORE PRACTICE

Respond with complete sentences, using the idioms as often as possible.

1. In what situation should you **think something over** before you make a
   decision?

2. How long did it take you to **come up with** a sentence for question 1?

3. Tell about a situation in which someone **called something off**.

4. You'd like to invite your friend to go to the beach with you. How can
   you do this, using **how about**?

5. Combine the sentences to make one sentence, using **as well**.

   a. Bob ate three sandwiches. Bob ate two apples.

   b. The Smiths have three cats. The Smiths have two dogs.

Lesson 15

I. DIALOGUE: In the Red

Nancy: Look at all these bills! How can we ever pay them?

  John: It's difficult to **make ends meet** these days. We'll have to **do without** something.

Nancy: OK, but what?

  John: Well, we can sell the car and use public transportation or walk.

Nancy: Isn't there any other way we can **cut down on** expenses?

  John: I don't think so. Selling the car is the only thing that will help **in the long run**.

Nancy: Let's **sleep on** it. Things always look better in the morning.

II. DEFINITIONS

make ends meet:

do without:

cut down on:

in the long run:

sleep on:

III. NOTES

cut down on: This idiom is often followed by a gerund (verb + *ing*).

> *Example:* I asked my daughter to cut down on **talking** on the tele-phone.

IV. STRUCTURE PRACTICE

Write the idioms in the spaces provided. Be sure the statements agree in person and tense. Some statements will be negative (−). You may change the form of the words in parentheses.

1. **(make) ends meet**

   a. They _____ last year by working very hard.

   b. She doesn't earn very much. How_____

   _____ she _____?

2. **(do) without**

   a. She _____ a car very easily. She takes the bus.

   b. They _____ a vacation last year in order to save money.

   c. I have _____ new shoes for a long time now.

3. **(cut) down on**

   a. "How does he save money?" "He_____

   _____ expenses by staying home a lot."

b. I have _____ smoking and I feel a lot
   better.

(−)c. If he _____ drinking, he will become
   an alcoholic.

4. **in the long run**

   a. _____, you will be healthier if you ex-
      ercise regularly.

   b. Although our team lost several games, they played very well

      _____.

5. **(sleep) on**

   a. It was a difficult decision, so I _____ it.

   b. I _____ this tonight and give you my
      decision tomorrow.

V. COMPREHENSION

Write the idioms from this lesson in the spaces provided. Be sure to use
the correct person and tense.

1. Richard is very hardworking, and I'm sure he'll be successful_____

   _____.

2. When Adam asked Eve to marry him, she told him she had to

   _____ it.

3. If you want to lose weight, you will have to_____

   _____ eating fried foods and desserts.

4. We can _____ a television. It's not necessary.

5. Jack couldn't _____, so his parents lent
   him some money to pay his rent.

6. The new president promised to _____ gov-
   ernment spending.

7. _____, it's better to study a little every day than to wait until just before the exam.

8. It's easy for me to _____ beef. I don't like it and I never eat it.

VI. MORE PRACTICE

Respond with complete sentences, using the idioms as often as possible.

1. **In the long run**, is it better to buy a house or rent an apartment? Why?

2. What should you **cut down on**?

3. How do you **make ends meet**? Is it difficult?

4. What is something you **do without** that you would like to have?

5. Your friend asks you to lend him a large amount of money. You'd like some time to think about it. What can you say to your friend, using **sleep on**?

Lesson 16

I. DIALOGUE: The Pack Rat

Ann: Would you **give me a hand** with this box?

Mary: Sure. Ugh . . . it's heavy! **No wonder** you couldn't lift it yourself. What's in it?

Ann: Oh, just some old clothes. I don't know what to do with them.

Mary: You know, you really should **get rid of** some of these things. You never wear them.

Ann: Okay. I think I'll start with this old sweater.

Mary: Hey! That's a very nice sweater. And look at this beautiful blouse! Can I **try them on**?

Ann: I have a good idea. Why don't you take the box home with you? That way you can **take your time** and look at everything.

II. DEFINITIONS

give someone a hand:

no wonder:

get rid of:

try on:

take one's time:

III. NOTES

try on: This idiom is a separable two-word verb.

> *Examples:* **Try on the shoes.**
> **Try the shoes on.**

When a pronoun is used, the verb must be separated.

> *Example:* **Try them on.**

IV. STRUCTURE PRACTICE

Write the idioms in the spaces provided. Be sure the statements agree in person and tense. Some statements will be negative (−). You may change the form of the words in parentheses.

1. **(give someone) a hand**

    a. Mary needs help. Let's _____.

    b. Bob moved last week and I _____.

    c. You look tired. I'll _____ with the dishes.

2. **no wonder**

    a. It's _____ he's always late for work. He doesn't have an alarm clock.

    b. Alice has five children. _____ she's always busy.

3. **(get) rid of**

    a. Joe's old car broke down, so he _____ it.

    b. Have you _____ those old magazines yet?

    c. She always _____ things she doesn't need.

4. **(try something) on—(try) on (something)**

   a. I _____ that coat, but I didn't buy it.

(−)b. Carol bought the wrong size dress because she_____

   _____.

   c. That shirt looks too big for you. _____

   you _____ before you bought it?

5. **(take one's) time**

   a. He eats very slowly. He _____.

(−)b. She makes a lot of mistakes because she_____

   _____.

   c. We spent all afternoon at the museum. We_____

   _____ and looked at everything.

V. COMPREHENSION

Write the idioms from this lesson in the spaces provided. Be sure to use the correct person and tense.

1. John sold his bicycle to Tom. He didn't want to_____

   _____ it, but he needed the money.

2. _____ you didn't pass the test. You didn't study.

3. My car was in the garage for a week. That mechanic really_____

   _____ fixing it.

4. I _____ five pairs of shoes before I found some that fit me.

5. You ate a whole box of chocolates. _____ you don't feel good.

6. We're going to paint the kitchen on Saturday. Would you like to

   _____?

7. I like to _____ when I go shopping. I don't like to hurry.

8. There's a dressing room in the corner of the store where you can _____ those pants.

VI. MORE PRACTICE

Respond with complete sentences, using the idioms as often as possible.

1. Describe a situation in which you **gave someone a hand**.

2. When was the last time you **tried something on**? What was it? Did it fit?

3. Your friend walked home in the rain without an umbrella. Now he is sick. What can you say to him, using **no wonder**?

4. What do you have at home that you should **get rid of**? How are you going to get **rid of it**?

5. In what situations do you like to **take your time**?

Give someone a hand

Review: Lessons 13–16

I. Write the best idiom from the following list in the space provided. Do not use the same idiom twice.

how about   **(sleep) on**
(make) friends   **in the long run**
as well   **(make) ends meet**
(try) on   **(cut) down on**
(think) over   **used to (verb)**

1. _____, I think we'll be happy that we moved to Pennsylvania.

2. _____ going to the movies with us?

3. I fixed a big dinner and baked a cake _____

   _____.

4. He _____ five coats, but he didn't buy one.

5. My sister enjoys parties and likes to _____

   _____.

6. The Smiths have a lot of money, but it's difficult for the Taylors to

   _____.

7. It's not easy to _____ expenses.

100

8. Barbara is an accountant now, but she_____

    _____ a dancer.

9. It's a good idea to _____ an important decision.

10. I can't decide today. I'll have to_____

    _____ it tonight.

II. Use the following idioms to complete the exercises. Do not use the
same idiom twice.

(give someone) a hand	**no wonder**
quite a few	**(do) without**
(take one's) time	**(come) up with**
(get) rid of	**(make) up (one's) mind**
(keep) (verb + *ing*)	**(call) off**

A. Rewrite the sentences, substituting idioms for the **boldface** words.

1. Lucy didn't want to **help us**.

   _____

2. The president of the club **canceled** the meeting.

   _____

3. **It's not surprising that** Jerry is so tall. His parents are both over
   six feet.

   _____

4. She **continued to read** after the others went to bed.

   _____

5. I finally **found** the answer to the problem.

   _____

B. Complete the conversations, using idioms and other words if necessary.

   1. A: "Do you always spend a lot of time reading the newspaper?"

      B: "Yes, I like to _____."

   2. A: "Are you going to throw that old meat in the garbage?"

      B: "Yes, I'm _____."

   3. A: "Have you decided yet?"

      B: "No, I _____."

   4. A: "I see that Peter has a lot of books."

      B: "Yes, he _____."

   5. A: "We don't have enough money left to buy cheese."

      B: "We'll have to _____."

Lesson 17

I. DIALOGUE: Crime Wave

Linda: Did you see this article in the newspaper? Two men **broke into** a house near here last night and took more than $3,000 in cash.

Ted: Did they **get away with** it?

Linda: Yes. The police are still looking for them.

Ted: That's nothing. A man **held up** my uncle on the street last week—in the middle of the afternoon!

Linda: Really? Where did that **take place**?

Ted: Only a block from here. Right in front of the post office.

Linda: **From now on**, I'm going to keep my money in the bank.

II. DEFINITIONS

break into:

get away with:

hold up:

take place:

from now on:

III. NOTES

hold up: This idiom is a separable two-word verb.

> *Examples:* The robbers **held the bank up**.
> The robbers **held up the bank**.

When a pronoun is used, the verb must be separated.

> *Example:* The robbers **held it up**.

This idiom is also used as a noun (**holdup**).

> *Example:* There was a **holdup** at the currency exchange yesterday.

hold up and **break into**: These idioms have different meanings. **Break into** describes a situation that may take place when no person other than the thief or thieves is present. **Hold up** occurs when at least one other person is present and the thief uses a weapon.

IV. STRUCTURE PRACTICE

Write the idioms in the spaces provided. Be sure the statements agree in person and tense. Some statements will be negative (−). You may change the form of the words in parentheses.

1. **(break) into**

   a. Burglars have _____ my aunt's house three times.

   b. Someone _____ my car and stole my tape player.

   c. John forgot his keys and had to _____ his own house.

2. **(get) away with**

   a. Tommy always _____ everything. His mother cannot believe anything bad about him.

(−)b. She stole a car, but she _____ it. She's in prison now.

3. **(hold something) up—(hold) up (something)**

   a. Jesse James and his gang _____ many banks in the nineteenth century.

(−)b. He said he was innocent and that he_____

   _____ the liquor store _____ .

4. **(take) place**

   a. The wedding _____ on July 17, 1964.

   b. The interviews will _____ on December 14.

   c. The state fair _____ every year in August.

5. **from now on**

   a. _____ , I'm going to drive more carefully.

   b. Fred promised his boss he'd work harder_____

   _____ .

IV. COMPREHENSION

Write the idioms from this lesson in the spaces provided. Be sure to use the correct person and tense.

1. The play *Romeo and Juliet* _____ in Italy.

2. Someone _____ the office in the middle of the night and stole the documents.

3. There were four customers there when the gunmen _____

   _____ the grocery store.

4. There is a change in the schedule. Class will begin at 8:00_____

_____.

5. While I was on vacation, someone _____
my apartment.

6. The 1984 Olympics _____ in Los Angeles.

7. The murderer _____ his crime. They
never found him.

8. The employees said that the man who _____
the store had a gun in each hand.

VI. MORE PRACTICE

Respond with complete sentences, using the idioms as often as possible.

1. What is something you're going to do **from now on**?

2. Is there a famous bandit in the history of your country? Who was he
and what or whom did he **hold up**?

3. What was the last movie you saw? Where did the story **take place**?

4. How can you make it more difficult for someone to **break into** your
house or apartment?

5. Tell about something you did when you were a child that was wrong.
Did you **get away with** it?

Lesson 18

I. DIALOGUE: Tomorrow Never Comes

Andrew: Have you written your term paper yet?

Ellen: No, but I'll have plenty of time to do it next week.

Andrew: That's what you said last week and the week before. You can't **put it off** forever. You should **take advantage of** your free time and do some work.

Ellen: The truth is, I've **fallen behind** in all my classes and I don't know if I can ever **catch up**.

Andrew: Well, talking about it won't help **at this point**.

Ellen: You're right. I'll start on it tomorrow.

Andrew: Not tomorrow! Today!

II. DEFINITIONS

put off:

take advantage of:

fall behind:

catch up:

at this point:

III. NOTES

put off: This idiom is a separable two-word verb.

> *Examples:* We decided to **put off our vacation** until June.
> We decided to **put our vacation off** until June.

When a pronoun is used, the verb must be separated.

> *Example:* We decided to **put it off** until June.

This idiom is often followed by a gerund (verb + *ing*).

> *Example:* Many people put off **paying** their taxes until the last moment.

IV. STRUCTURE PRACTICE

Write the idioms in the spaces provided. Be sure the statements agree in person and tense. Some statements will be negative (−). You may change the form of the words in parentheses.

1. **(put something) off — (put) off (something)**

   a. He always _____ going to the dentist. He doesn't like to go.

   b. She was very busy that week, so she _____ _____ the party _____ .

   c. I have _____ buying new shoes for a long time.

2. **(take) advantage of**

   a. We _____ the beautiful weather and went to the park.

(−)b. Many people _____ the cultural activities in the city. They never go to the museums, concerts, and theaters.

   c. She saves money because she _____ sales to buy things at low prices.

3. **(fall) behind**

   a. The Smiths _____ in their mortgage payments and lost their house.

(−)b. I _____ in my homework. I'll study every night.

4. **(catch) up**

   a. Joe worked very hard and _____ with the rest of the class.

   b. I'd like to _____ on reading during my vacation.

   c. She _____ on her housework every weekend.

5. **at this point**

   a. _____, Jennifer and Stan haven't decided when they're going to get married.

   b. The score is 8 to 8. _____, no one is winning the game.

V. COMPREHENSION

Write the idioms from this lesson in the spaces provided. Be sure to use the correct person and tense.

1. The policeman ran as fast as he could, but he couldn't_____ _____ with the burglar.

2. The factory _____ in production, so everyone had to work overtime.

3. _____, I don't have enough money to buy a car. I hope I can get one next year.

4. They _____ the wedding because the bride's mother was sick.

5. Ken had to work late, so we _____ eating dinner until he arrived.

6. You can borrow books from the library for free. You should _____ _____ it.

7. The little boy couldn't walk as fast as the others, and he soon _____.

8. The Whites _____ the low interest rates and borrowed money to buy a house.

VI. MORE PRACTICE

Respond with complete sentences, using the idioms as often as possible.

1. Make two sentences about yourself, using **at this point**.

2. How are you going to **take advantage of** your vacation?

3. What's something you often **put off** doing?

4. Have you ever **fallen behind** in something? What was it?

5. Did you **catch up**? (See question 4.) How?

Lesson 19

I. DIALOGUE: A Missing Person

Dan: Please help me. I thought my little brother was right behind me, but **all of a sudden** when I looked back he wasn't there.

Salesperson: He probably **got lost** in the crowd. There are a lot of shoppers in the store today. What does he **have on**?

Dan: A yellow jacket and blue pants. He's only four.

Salesperson: I think I see him near the elevators. Does he have red hair and freckles?

Dan: Yes, that's him. Thank goodness!

Salesperson: Don't **let go of** his hand after this.

Dan: Don't worry. I'll **keep an eye on** him.

II. DEFINITIONS

all of a sudden:

get lost:

have on:

let go of:

keep an eye on:

III. NOTES

have on: This idiom is a separable two-word verb.

Examples: I **have on** my shoes.
I **have** my shoes **on**.

When a pronoun is used, the verb must be separated.

Example: I **have** them **on**.

IV. STRUCTURE PRACTICE

Write the idioms in the spaces provided. Be sure the statements agree in person and tense. Some statements will be negative (−). You may change the form of the words in parentheses.

1. **all of a sudden**

   a. _____, it began to rain and we hurried inside.

   b. Everyone stopped talking _____ when the president entered the room.

2. **(get) lost**

   a. He _____ every time he drives in a strange city.

   b. The dog _____ and they never found him.

   (−)c. We _____ because we had a good map.

3. **(have) on (something)—(have something) on**

   a. She _____ her best clothes _____ .

   b. Do you see him? He _____ a white sweater.

(−)c. I couldn't see a thing because I _____

my glasses _____.

4. **(let) go of**

(−)a. The man caught the thief and _____
him until the police came.

b. Please _____ my arm. You're hurting
me.

5. **(keep) an eye on**

a. Bob _____ the children while Joan
went to the bank.

b. Will you _____ my apartment while
I'm out of town?

c. She always _____ her purse.

V. COMPREHENSION

Write the idioms from this lesson in the spaces provided. Be sure to use
the correct person and tense.

1. The man in front of me _____ the door
and it shut in my face.

2. The Martins _____ and had to ask for directions at a gas station.

3. If you take Teddy to the pool, be sure to_____

_____ him. He can't swim.

4. Pam _____ on her way to the airport and
missed her flight.

5. _____ a man ran into the theater and
shouted, "Fire!"

6. Brenda's mother told her she _____ too
much makeup.

7. I'll lend you my camera if you promise to_____

_____ it. It's very expensive.

8. I was surprised when Lynn began to cry_____

_____.

VI. MORE PRACTICE

Respond with complete sentences, using the idioms as often as possible.

1. Have you ever **gotten lost**? Where were you and what happened?

2. a. What do you **have on** today?

   b. What does the person next to you **have on**?

   c. What did you **have on** yesterday?

3. What or whom do you **keep an eye on**? Why?

4. Describe something that happened **all of a sudden**.

5. You are learning to ice skate and your friend is holding your arm. What can you say to him or her, using **let go of**?

Lesson 20

I. DIALOGUE: Practice Makes Perfect

Charles: Did you say *ice*?

Rita: No, I said *eyes*. Sometimes I have **quite a bit of** trouble with pronunciation.

Charles: Oh, *eyes* and *ice*. It's easy to **mix them up**.

Rita: Yes, the difference between them is really difficult for me, **not to mention** words like *cap* and *cup*. I often can't **tell them apart**.

Charles: **Even so**, it'll be easier for you when you've been in the United States longer.

Rita: I hope you're right.

Charles: I'm sure of it!

II. DEFINITIONS

quite a bit of:

mix up:

not to mention:

tell apart:

even so:

III. NOTES

quite a bit (of): This idiom is used with noncount nouns.

> *Example:*   We have quite a bit of **time (money, sugar, tea,** etc.).

It is not used in negative statements. The negative form is **not much**.

> *Example:*   We have quite a bit of furniture, but we do**n't** have **much** space.

When this idiom occurs at the end of a sentence, it is simply **quite a bit**.

> *Example:*   Mrs. Sullivan's back hurts **quite a bit**.

mix up: This is a separable two-word verb.

> *Examples:* I always **mix up Tuesday and Thursday**.
> I always **mix Tuesday and Thursday up**.

When a pronoun is used, the verb must be separated.

> *Example:*   I always **mix them up**.

IV. STRUCTURE PRACTICE

Write the idioms in the spaces provided. Be sure the statements agree in person and tense. Some statements will be negative (−). You may change the form of the words in parentheses.

1. **quite a bit (of)**

    a. My friend didn't enjoy the movie, but I liked it _____

    _____ .

    b. We studied _____ grammar in that class.

    c. That big car uses _____ gas.

2. **(mix things) up—(mix) up (things)**

(−)a. The new teacher knows our names already. I'm surprised that she

_____.

    b. I wanted to call Sam, but I dialed Joe's number. I often_____

_____ their numbers.

    c. Donna _____ the dates and thought
the meeting was on the fifteenth.

3. **not to mention**

    a. I have to pay the rent, the electricity, and the gas bill,_____

_____ the phone bill.

    b. Mrs. Wong is active in many clubs and organizations,_____

_____ the church.

4. **(tell things/people) apart**

    a. My sister and I are twins. Many people can't_____

_____.

    b. Ben's dogs all look the same to me. I don't know how he_____

_____.

5. **even so**

    a. English is difficult for me. _____, my
English has improved.

    b. Chicago is big and noisy and has terrible weather. _____

_____, it's my home and I love it.

V. COMPREHENSION

Write the idioms from this lesson in the spaces provided. Be sure to use
the correct person and tense.

1. We _____ the directions and took the
wrong road.

2. Only an expert could _____ the original painting and
the copy _____.

3. He has _____ money in the bank.

4. She sleeps a lot. _____, she's always tired.

5. I didn't eat much, but my brother ate _____

_____.

6. Only the twins' mother can _____.

7. Rachel speaks French and Russian, _____
Portuguese.

8. I put the letters in the wrong envelopes. I_____

_____.

VI. MORE PRACTICE

Respond with complete sentences, using the idioms as often as possible.

1. What are some things you often **mix up**?

2. Make three sentences, using **quite a bit (of)**.

3. What words in English are, or were, difficult for you to **tell apart**?

4. Rewrite the sentences, adding **even so**.

   a. I work very hard. I like my job.

   b. I'm not a very good dancer. I enjoy dancing.

5. Reword the sentences, using **not to mention**.

    a. Don is a good swimmer, an excellent tennis player, and a very good golfer.

    b. For homework, we had to read two chapters of the book, do four grammar exercises, and write a composition.

Keep an eye on

Review: Lessons 17–20

I. Match the numbers and letters to make statements using idioms. Write the statements below and underline the idioms.

1. The meeting will	a. that book quite a bit.
2. All of a sudden,	b. I'm going to read more.
3. He had on	c. we heard a loud noise.
4. From now on,	d. held up the bank.
5. My mother asked me to	e. a pair of purple boots.
6. Two men wearing ski masks	f. I've finished half my work.
7. We should take advantage of	g. take place in Frank's office.
	h. the nice weather and have a picnic.
8. I can't tell	i. butter and margarine apart.
9. At this point,	j. keep an eye on my little sister.
10. I liked	

1. _____

2. _____

3. _____

4. _____

5. _____

6. _____

7. _____

8. _____

9. _____

10. _____

II. Write the best idiom from the following list in the space provided. Do not use the same idiom twice.

> **not to mention** **(let) go of**
> **(mix) up**   **even so**
> **(put) off**   **(get) lost**
> **(break) into**   **(catch) up**
> **(get) away with** **(fall) behind**

1. I _____ and had to ask a man on the street where I was.

2. Someone _____ our hotel room and stole our airline tickets.

3. John _____ in his classes and had to ask his teachers for help.

4. I _____ the hot potato quickly.

5. Our team is very good. _____, I don't think they'll win.

6. I often _____ *much* and *many*. What's the difference between them?

7. I was sick for a week and now I'm trying to _____ _____ on my work.

8. The Carsons have three dogs and two cats, _____ _____ an aquarium full of fish.

9. I didn't _____ parking there. The policeman gave me a ticket.

10. I don't like to do laundry, so I sometimes _____ _____ washing my clothes.

Crossword Puzzle: Lessons 1–20

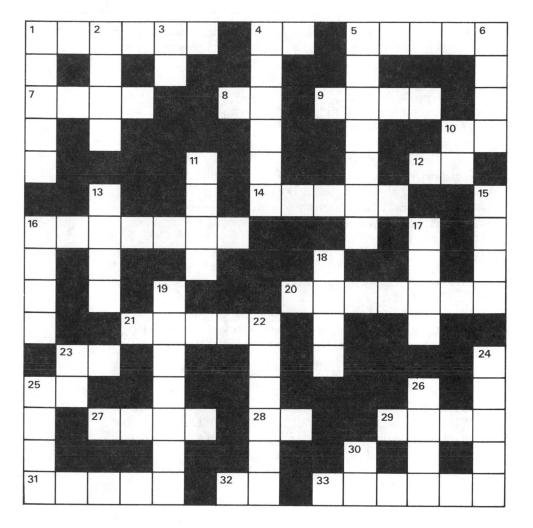

ACROSS

1. Mrs. Jones is in _____ of the customer service department.
4. We don't know who was _____ blame for the accident.
5. Do you know how I can get in _____ with Carolyn?
7. I'll have to brush _____ _____ the rules before we play bridge.
8. I _____ out of coffee, so I'll drink tea instead.
9. In the _____ run, we'll save money by buying food in quantity.
10. _____' better study hard if I want to pass that exam.

12. When he arrived in the United States he didn't speak English _____ all.
14. Please mail this letter _____ away. It's very important.
16. We bought our airline tickets two months in _____.
20. I'm really looking _____ to the holidays.
21. Dan doesn't like to _____ up. He usually wears jeans.
23. I'll take you home. It isn't out of _____ way.
25. The doctor says Irene will _____ up and about soon.
27. It's not unusual for managers to _____ fault with their employees.
28. This coat is still good. I can _____ without a new one.
29. Our boss is going to _____ the bill for the office party.
31. My husband and I take _____ doing the dishes.
32. Darling, I fell _____ love with you the first time we met.
33. No _____ your eyes hurt. You need glasses.

DOWN

1. I can usually _____ on my uncle to lend me money.
2. Will you keep _____ eye _____ the children while I cook dinner?
3. It was touch and _____, but I think I passed the test.
4. Be careful with Mr. Brown. He loses his _____ very easily.
5. Grace _____ it over and decided not to get married.
6. Thank you for giving me a _____ with the laundry.
10. We usually take _____ easy on the weekends.
11. The movie starts at 8:00, so I'll _____ you up at 7:30.
13. It took him two weeks to get _____ his cold.
15. When did you _____ out about George's accident?
16. There were quite _____ _____ people at the park yesterday.
17. Some people think they can get _____ with breaking the law.
18. We got _____ and had to ask a policeman for directions.
19. I only lived in New York for six months, so I didn't make many _____ there.
22. All of a _____ I remembered my appointment with the dentist.
23. Anne let _____ down when she forgot her promise to help me.
24. Victor takes _____ his mother in personality.
25. I do my _____ to be a good parent.
26. The robbers planned to _____ up the First National Bank.
30. This semester I'm taking biology and chemistry, not _____ mention physics.

Appendix: Dialogue Titles

Lesson 1: "Easier said than done" describes something that is more difficult to do than to talk about.

Lesson 2: We use "like father, like son" to refer to a boy or man who is like his father in behavior or personality. We can also say "like mother, like daughter".

Lesson 3: To "get in shape" is to become in good physical condition by exercising, eating good food, and so on.

Lesson 4: "Robbing Peter to pay Paul" is borrowing money from one source to pay another. A person who does this remains in debt.

Lesson 5: "A question of money" is a problem or difficulty concerning money.

Lesson 6: A "family feud" is a continuing quarrel between two families or two branches of the same family. The feud between the families of Shakespeare's Romeo and Juliet is an example.

Lesson 7: "A man or woman of his or her word" is a person who keeps promises, someone you can trust or depend on.

Lesson 8: "Duty calls" describes a situation in which one must fulfill one's obligations to family, work, country, and so on.

Lesson 9: To have "a foot in the door" is to have a special chance or opportunity, usually for a job, because of someone one knows.

Lesson 10:   "First things first" means that the most important things should be done before others.

Lesson 11:   To give someone "a taste of his or her own medicine" is to treat that person as he or she treats others, especially when the treatment is unpleasant.

Lesson 12:   "Last-minute notice" describes a situation in which someone is given little or no time to prepare for something.

Lesson 13:   "No one is an island" suggests that no person can live completely apart from others. The original quotation is from a poem by John Donne (English poet, 1572–1631): "No man is an island, entire of itself. . . ."

Lesson 14:   A "potluck" is a meal to which each of the guests brings a dish that he or she prepared at home. Most often, no one knows what kind of food will be served until the guests have arrived and uncovered their dishes.

Lesson 15:   To be "in the red" is to be in debt, or to owe more money than one has. "In the black" is the opposite.

Lesson 16:   A "pack rat" is an animal that lives in the southwest of the United States and carries to its home small things that it finds. We use "pack rat" to describe a person who collects and saves things in the same way.

Lesson 17:   A "crime wave" is a series of crimes, one after the other, in the same area, usually within a short period of time.

Lesson 18:   "Tomorrow never comes" describes the fact that tomorrow is always in the future and can never be today. We use it to say that if something isn't done now, it might never be done.

Lesson 19:   "A missing person" is someone who is lost and cannot be located by his or her family or friends.

Lesson 20:   "Practice makes perfect" expresses the idea that with practice, performance or ability will improve.

Index/Glossary

after all (page 52): used to introduce a reason or explanation.

> *Let's go to a movie. After all, it's Saturday night.*

all of a sudden (page 114): suddenly, without warning.

> *All of a sudden, a little girl ran in front of the truck.*

as well (page 84): also, too.

> *David speaks English, Arabic, and French as well.*

at all (page 7): in the smallest amount.

> *The doctor told him not to eat any sugar at all.*

at this point (page 109): at this time.

> *At this point, I've saved five hundred dollars for my vacation.*

be about to (page 52): be ready to do something.

> *The baby was about to fall down the stairs when I caught her.*

be better off (page 58): be in a better situation.

> *I will be better off when I move into my new apartment.*

be broke (page 17): be without money.

> *I paid all my bills and now I'm broke.*

be in charge of (page 52): be responsible for.

> *Mrs. Baker is in charge of the family's finances.*

be out of (page 70): be without something one had before.

   I can't make sandwiches because we're out of bread.

be out of shape (page 12): be in poor condition.

   He is out of shape because he doesn't exercise.

be to blame (page 58): be responsible for something wrong.

   George is to blame for his poor grades. He never studies.

be touch and go (page 65): be uncertain of a result.

   It was touch and go, but the plane landed safely.

be up and about (page 65): be out of bed and active after an illness.

   Carol has been very sick. It will be a long time before she's up and about.

be up to someone (page 27): be one's decision or responsibility.

   We can meet tomorrow or Wednesday. It's up to you.

be used to (page 65): be accustomed to.

   Juan is from Colombia, so he's used to hot weather.

break into (page 104): enter by force.

   Burglars broke into the warehouse and stole $20,000 worth of appliances.

brush up on (page 2): review, study again.

   I need to brush up on the rules before we play bridge.

by heart (page 2): by memorizing.

   An actor must learn his lines by heart.

by the way (page 70): some added information.

   The meeting will be next Tuesday. By the way, Mr. Hughes will be there.

call off (page 84): cancel.

   We called off our party because of the storm.

catch up (page 109): become not behind.

   I missed two weeks of class. I'll have to work hard to catch up.

come up with (page 84): find an answer, idea, plan.

   The president asked his advisors to come up with a plan for improving relations with the unions.

count on someone (page 37): depend on someone.

> *Sandra counts on her neighbor to drive her to work.*

cut down on (page 90): reduce.

> *Joan cut down on eating in restaurants to save money.*

do one's best (page 32): try as hard as possible.

> *I do my best to finish my work.*

do something over (page 58): do something again.

> *The doctor couldn't believe the results of the blood test, so he did it over to be sure.*

do without (page 90): live without.

> *We did without electricity and running water on our camping trip.*

dress up (page 27): put on one's best clothes.

> *We usually dress up for weddings and funerals.*

drop off (page 42): take somewhere, deliver.

> *I'll drop off your shoes at the repair shop tomorrow.*

even so (page 119): nevertheless, however, but.

> *Jane is overweight. Even so, she's very attractive.*

every other (page 12): every alternate, every second thing in a series.

> *I call my sister every other week.*

fall behind (page 109): do something more slowly than expected.

> *The child fell behind in learning to read, so the teacher gave him extra help.*

fall in love (page 70): begin to love.

> *Joe fell in love with Karen soon after he met her.*

find fault with (page 58): criticize.

> *Whenever he goes to a restaurant, Mr. Higgins finds fault with the food and service.*

find out (page 52): learn or discover.

> *He was very happy when he found out he got an A on the exam.*

foot the bill (page 27): pay.

Our supervisor footed the bill for the office picnic.

from now on (page 104): beginning now and continuing in the future.

I promise to write you a letter every week from now on.

get along with (page 32): have good relations.

Mrs. Cooper asked her children to stop fighting and try to get along with each other.

get away with (page 104): do something wrong and not be caught.

They never found the bank robber. He got away with his crime.

get in touch with (page 52): contact, communicate with.

You can get in touch with me by telephone. My number is 549-2985.

get lost (page 114): lose one's way or direction.

It's easy to get lost in a strange city.

get over (page 65): become normal again after an illness or bad experience.

Patty was bitten once and has never gotten over her fear of dogs.

get rid of (page 95): dispose of.

I finally got rid of my son's baby clothes last week. He's fourteen now.

get together (page 12): come together, meet.

I got together with my friends on my birthday.

give someone a hand (page 95): help someone.

Let me give you a hand with those packages.

give up (page 2): stop or abandon doing something.

Frank had to give up swimming because of an ear infection.

go Dutch (page 27): a situation in which each person pays for his or her own food or entertainment.

I often eat lunch in a restaurant with my friends and we always go Dutch.

go out (page 70): go to parties, movies, restaurants, and other social activities.

Mel likes to go out and have a good time.

go to pieces (page 7): lose control of one's emotions.

Mr. Wilson went to pieces when the fire destroyed his house.

had better (page 17): should.

You had better drive more carefully.

have got (page 17): have.

We have got a lot of bills to pay.

have on (page 114): be wearing.

Al felt strange because he had on a suit and the others had on jeans.

hold up (page 104): rob, using a weapon.

Several men held up the passengers on the train.

how about (page 84): used to ask for information.

How about fish for dinner?

in advance (page 42): before.

I made my appointment with the doctor two weeks in advance.

in the long run (page 90): in the end, as a final result.

In the long run, it's a good idea to save a little money every week.

in time (page 42): soon enough.

I like to get up in time to take a shower before I leave for school.

keep an eye on (page 114): watch, guard, take care of.

Kathy asked her roommate to keep an eye on the cake in the oven while she took a bath.

keep someone company (page 65): stay with or accompany someone.

Please come in the kitchen and keep me company while I cook dinner.

keep (verb + *ing*) (page 79): continue doing something.

I keep forgetting to buy shampoo. I must do it today.

let go of (page 114): release something one is holding.

Mark let go of the books and they fell to the floor.

let someone down (page 37): disappoint someone.

My cousin let me down when he didn't come to my wedding.

let someone know (page 37): inform someone.

> *If you let me know what time your train will arrive, I'll meet you at the station.*

look forward to (page 12): think about something in the future with pleasure.

> *She's looking forward to having her baby next month.*

lose one's temper (page 32): become very angry.

> *The director lost his temper and shouted at the actors.*

make ends meet (page 90): have enough money to live or to pay one's bills.

> *Louise has to work at two jobs to make ends meet.*

make friends (page 79): become friends.

> *Margaret makes friends everywhere she goes.*

make fun of (page 2): laugh at, joke about.

> *The boys make fun of the dog's long ears.*

make sense (page 17): be logical, be reasonable.

> *It makes sense to buy a small car. You will save money on gas.*

make up (page 32): become friends again after an argument or fight.

> *Children usually make up with their friends quickly after fights.*

make up one's mind (page 79): decide.

> *Sally made up her mind to study engineering.*

mix up (page 119): confuse.

> *The mailman sometimes mixes up my neighbor's mail and mine.*

no wonder (page 95): it's not surprising that.

> *You were at the beach all day. No wonder you are sunburned.*

not to mention (page 119): in addition to.

> *I like to read biographies and mysteries, not to mention science fiction.*

on purpose (page 37): as the result of a plan, intentionally.

> *The Crawfords were very angry when they learned that the neighbors' son had hit their cat on purpose.*

on second thought (page 27): after thinking again.

> *On second thought, the Franklins decided not to join the club.*

out of one's way (page 42): away from the direction in which one is going or normally goes.

I drove twenty miles out of my way to take Helen home.

pick up (page 42): take away from a place.

The rescue helicopter picked up seven of the passengers after the plane crash.

put off (page 109): postpone, change to a later date.

I'll have to put off buying a new coat until I have more money.

quite a bit of (page 119): much.

We've prepared quite a bit of food for our guests.

quite a few (page 79): many.

There were quite a few people at the reception.

right away (page 17): immediately.

I couldn't see the doctor right away. I had to wait.

run into (page 70): meet by chance.

I ran into an old friend on the train this morning.

see eye to eye (page 32): agree, have the same opinion.

Mr. and Mrs. O'Connor see eye to eye on everything except politics.

show up (page 37): arrive, appear.

The reporters were disappointed when the movie star didn't show up for the interview.

sleep on (page 90): postpone a decision, usually until the next day.

The mayor asked the city council to sleep on the plan and to vote on it the next day.

stand out (page 58): be noticeable.

Leonardo da Vinci stood out as an artistic and scientific genius.

take advantage of (page 109): use for one's own benefit.

We should take advantage of the sale and buy furniture now.

take after (page 7): be like someone in one's family in appearance or personality.

Linda takes after her mother. They are both tall and thin.

take it easy (page 7): relax, be calm.

   We like to take it easy on Sundays.

take one's time (page 95): do something slowly.

   I like to take my time when I prepare dinner for guests.

take place (page 104): happen.

   American presidential elections always take place in November.

take turns (page 7): alternate doing something with one or more people.

   Young children have to learn to take turns with each other when playing games.

tell apart (page 119): see or know the difference.

   Dan and his brother sound so much alike that I can't tell their voices apart.

think over (page 84): consider carefully.

   It's a good idea to spend some time thinking it over before you get married.

try on (page 95): test for fit.

   You should try on shoes before you buy them.

used to (verb) (page 79): something one did in the past, but not now.

   He used to work in a department store, but now he's a bank teller.

what's the matter (page 2): what's wrong? What's the problem?

   What's the matter with the baby? She's been crying all day.

would rather (page 12): prefer to.

   I would rather go to the ballet than to the opera.